How

Are

You?

I'm Alive,

Blessed, and

Challenged!

PART ONE

How Are You?

I'm Alive, Blessed, and Challenged!

SHARLIENE PHILLIPS

Self-published by Sharliene Phillips

First Edition, 2025

Copyright © 2025 by Sharliene Phillips
All rights reserved

Cover design and Interior design by Ian Koviak

ISBN Paperback: 979-8-9989612-8-1
ISBN Hardcover: 979-8-9989612-7-4
ISBN e-Book: 979-8-9989612-5-0
ISBN Audiobook: 979-8-9989612-6-7

Printed in the United States of America

Dedication

To family, friends, and therapists,
for without their love and
support this book would not have
been made.

To my sister/mother/best friend
thank you so much for
everything you are
You will always be my hero:
I love you.

To my parents. We have a lot of
issues, but you chose to bring
me into this world and for that I
thank you and I love you.

Lastly, to the future: you terrify me, and I do not know what is next, but I know I cannot wait.

Trigger Warning

Thank you so much for giving my book a read! Please read the trigger warning before continuing and I hope you enjoy!

This book contains sensitive material such as:

Sexual assault,

Depression,

Anxiety attacks,

Panic attacks,

Self-harm,

And possibly more.

So please remember to practice self-care before, during, and after reading.

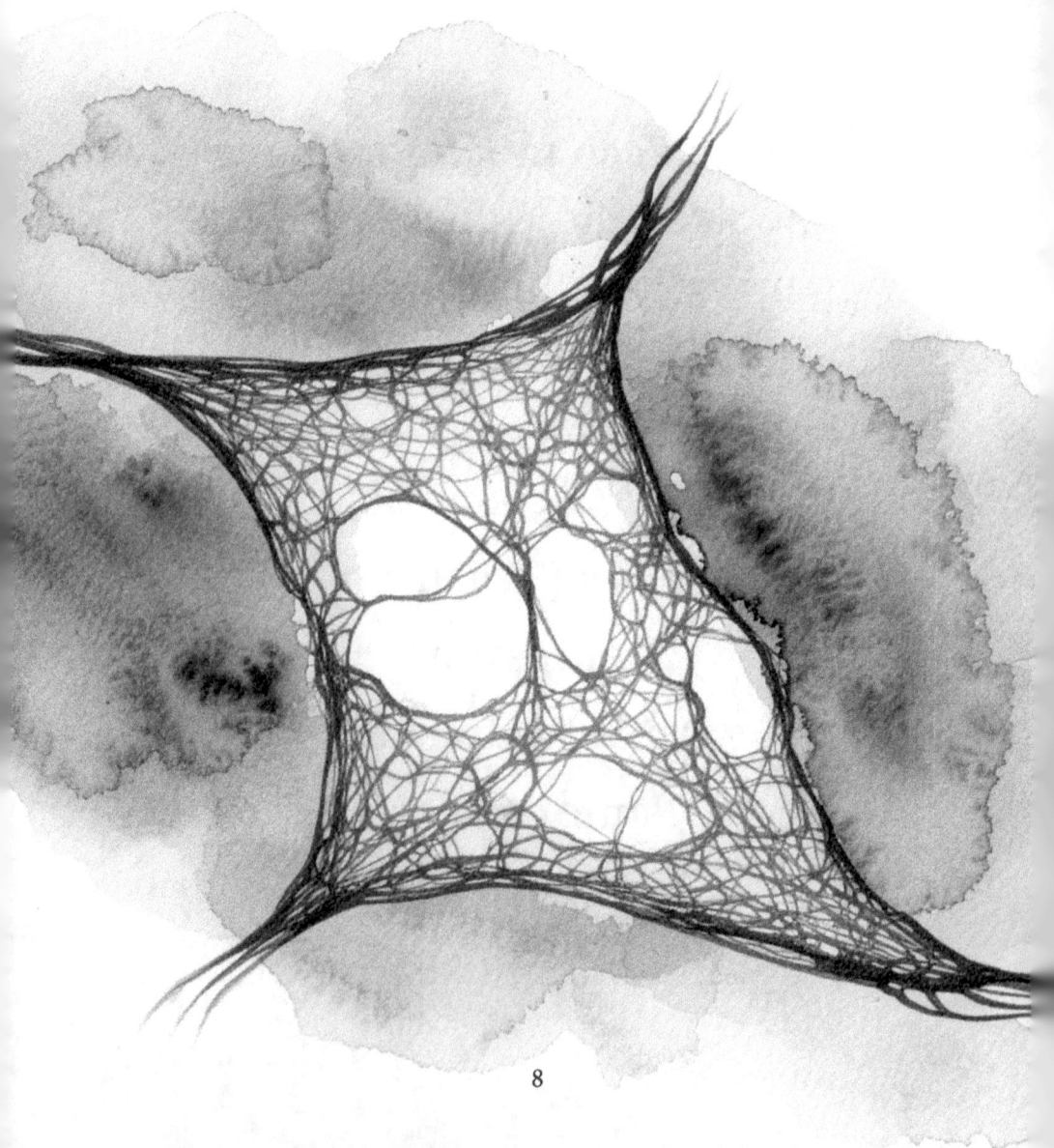

I Know Why I Write

I write...

So, I know I am strong.

So, I know I am not the same person as each new letter forms the words that help me to elaborately convey my soul.

So, I know that when I feel like a completely questionable how-are-you-still-alive-waste-of-space over ninety-nine percent of the time, that other one percent is cheering for me to stay strong and to get stronger, braver, and smarter.

So, I can remind myself every
day that I am not alone and that
I have people that care about me
even when I forget that they
do and that I need to.

So, I just know and know more.

So, I remember to not
only remember,
but to move forward, and when
I fall, make sure I notice
everything as I fall, and when
I hit the ground, or the
bottom of the hole,
I get back up and move forward.

I Am Here

The more you tell me I am not
a waist of space, the more every
inch of me feels like it is made of
unfamiliar and uncomfortable
layers that I cannot wait to shed.

I try to be human or normal
or even sane, but it is
impossible for me.

The more I try, the more shit just
keeps piling up, and I try to play
catch up, but that is all I am
doing is catching up.

I want to be caught up already

or even just know what that feels like.

People get tired of me whining about almost being kidnapped more than once, about being raped multiple times, about being in abusive relationships, about being abused in so many ways throughout my life a psychopathic killer would want to adopt me just to protect me—, but hold on it doesn't stop there. Do the words self-harm, sexual assault, sexual harassment, physical assault, attempted murder, stalking, depression, anxiety, post-traumatic stress disorder, panic attacks, agoraphobia, and so much more, mean anything to

you? because to me they mean,
God bless you.

You're still alive because you
are writing this poem.

Oh! Here I am whining and over
sharing again, right, because
being vulnerable is only okay
when the person is paid to listen
to you, but they don't always
give a damn about you or your
problems; just as long as you
come in, so they can get a sign
off on their paycheck.

Please don't insult my scars or
slay my emotional state of self-
degradation with the words that
say you care. Is more what you
want to know? Because I will not
hesitate to bring you back down

to the level you thought you left me at to grovel and relinquish all sense of brain activity you just assumed I had let go of because you see me as beneath you, yet if you take time to analyze your mind and realize that while I might be a list of unhealthy, unstable, intolerable sack-of-symptoms, labels, and reasons, then we have always been on the same level. Between being born and dying there is only one level and we all share it.

So, the answer to your question is no,
you don't have to keep listening.
You can go ahead and let your eyes glaze over or pull out your

phone, but note the sound
of my voice because it may be
small, but you will finally hear
what I have to say because
I am not done yet.

World (I understand)

I fell in love with you from the
moment I opened my eyes and
saw you. So many wonders
were held in you, so many
stories shared and unshared,
so many breaths still left to be
found explored and cherished.
I thought of you as this big,
golden, wonderous, illuminating,
everlasting glory, even though
when we met, I did not even
know what those words meant.

Hell, I did not even know what words were. However, you have enlightened me to your true nature and enveloped me as if I were a bird attempting to take flight, but somehow forgot that you cut my fucking wings off and stripped me of everything that has built me into this person I can no longer recognize. Not knowing if that is a good or a bad thing. But... I still called you by your name to give you some semblance of your humanity because calling you less than would make me no better than those who came before me, who failed to realize this concept, for you are called world and I shall treat you as such because I know what it is like to have everything in you stolen and replaced with something someone said was okay, something someone said would keep you warm, something someone said would give you yourself back, something someone said yes, that is it. Someone else said something, but I do not recall them being you or I. So, stop standing in everyone's shadow including your own. Helpful is helpful but standing on your own is how we learn to survive when we have everything and when we have nothing.

Encouragement
to Be a Better Person

I see the last five dollars slip from
your hand into a stranger's cup.

You don't hear the true thank you,
but maybe I am wrong.

Due to the fact that you do the
same thing every day on your
way home from wherever you
have been that day.

I saw you at the store when
you had to put everything back
because the moths that flew from

your back pocket as you removed your wallet and saw nothing.

I stepped out of line and said I will pay for you not because I felt sorry for you. No, that is not the case at all! So many people looking around asking why? I grab the cashier's microphone and say this person's last five dollars goes with a stranger every single day whether it is the same person as the day before or another new person gone from stranger to friend—, so, ladies and gentlemen, does that answer your questions?

This person is an encouragement of what we all should and could be. As the dollars slip from my hand, I see more transformed hearts reach into this person's hands and say thank you for the encouragement to help me be a human being that gives a damn about more than just myself.

I'm Sorry

When I was little my mom told me never say sorry because you're not a sorry person, but as I got older, I realized that me and my mom are similar in some ways, but this is not one of them.

So, when someone says they are sorry, don't tell them I know who you are or you don't really mean it. Tell them, if they are truly sorry, then show you.

Saying sorry does not mean you are weak or that you're a sorry person who is unworthy of being forgiven. It means you realized the pain you caused the other person and can only hope that one day they can forgive you and that you can earn their trust back.

Accepting an I'm sorry doesn't mean you're stupid even if you accept it a hundred times. It just means you can see through the pain to forgive and allow yourself to heal.

Happiness

It is truly joyous when the day wakes us up to all of the new wonders of the world, whether they be good or bad: take them in and change them, bend them, keep them the same, or completely remake them if you wish and have a pleasant day.

I mean each time you hear a laughing smile coming from deep in a baby's heart, you think back on what that was like.

Or even just daydream for a little while until your mouth drops open and your favorite song just pours out of you as you start singing and dancing not caring whose watching.

And that, my brothers and sisters, is just a portion of the different types of moments that make up what I presume to be true happiness... Or is that just my opinion? If so, please tell me some of the things that make you truly happy.

Rainbow Community

We are happy.

We can love.

We are happy that we can love
who we want.

We are happy.

We can be in love.

We are happy that we can be
in love with who we want.

We are happy... no... wait that's
been done and used, so let me
rearrange your mind, so these

words just fall in.

Lesbian, Gay, Bisexual, Transgender, Queer, Questioning, Intersex, Asexual, Allies, Pan sexual, and much more.

They are not just a sign-sealed, hand-delivered set of labels stamped with an abbreviation.

It is not a cry for attention.

It is not a phase.

Furthermore, we are all human and we are all different, so stop judging and start asking.

We may not have come stereo typically into this world as...

Glittery, well-dressed weight benches, wearing a plaid question mark as a birthmark with a little

something extra saying—not just
sex, but—no sex, wrong sex, no
labels, I like both, screaming I
like penises and have one too,
shouting I like vagina and what
do you know I have one too,
or we just support.

We know who we are, and we are
happy with who we are.

Truth Is All You Wan.

Truth is all you want and sometimes along the way it is hard to find that anywhere.

So many people give the impression that the truth is what they say it is or it is what you want it to be or so many other people's descriptions of definitions come in to play, but you don't believe that.

For as a child you were told that honesty is always the best policy

and always tell the truth
even if it hurts.

However, as you get older you
realize that even that was a lie—
no one cares what you have to say.

Until.

One day you snap and say no
more lies.

I want the truth.

You may not believe I am
worth the truth, but I am here
to tell you that I am.

So.

Tell me the truth.

It's all I want.

Today or Tomorrow
I Am Okay

Today or tomorrow.

Vice versa.

We come here and seek a way,
a meaning, anything to a when,
where, why, who.

For the love of humanity.

What is going on?

I should, I could, but I don't...
know.

I am pretty sure I have
never ever been okay.

I just say one of the lines my
feelings are forced to use to cloak
themselves in secrets and lies, so
if you ask me how I am.

I scream in silence,
but say I'm okay.

Signed Cracked
Never Broken

In the moments where I am
happy, I am extremely happy, but
most moments I feel like all of me
is being ripped bare and laid out
like a corpse in a shallow grave,
calling me, taunting me, telling
me everything I already know
to be true or false.

It's never taken lightly that I may
not listen or even when I do,
I still feel the seconds upon days

of highlighted anger, grief, and
despair: those days are in,
but I am not.

My mind, my body, my soul, and
my breath are no longer a part of
me. They are moving, squirming
underneath a rock of a mountain,
and me, screaming sad whispers,
trying not to let a drop fall, for
I know once it does, more are
to come. I am so filled with hate
and regret when the word stop
actually means go.

You know me, ha! If you knew the
breath of a little girl was the same
as that of a teenager grown into
a woman,then you'd know that
being used is nothing new.

When you confused stop with go

and broke the trust whatever was
left from that first time and so
many chances before—, it wasn't
just the stop and go, or no and
yes. You twisted some part of you
must have known that deep down
you and I were not anywhere close
to being on the same page.

While I sit in shame and your life
of lies and deception goes on.
I know, and you know everything.

Consensual is just a word to you.
A definition in a book with no use
to you and was in no way a part of
that night. So please don't
even look at me. If you see
me or if you dare

come close to hurt or damage me,
just know my lungs will sing.

You raped me.
I thought love, care, and
friendship would come,
but reality sat in.

So once again fear is a word I
was branded with, but strength,
courage, and grace are
what I gained.

I might be cracked,
but I am never broken.

Sleepy Nightmare

Sleep, sleep, sleep she cries as
she sits at the edge of her bed,
knowing that it will never claim
her the same again.

She fidgets with her pillow while
a head attached to a body gasps
for air and shakes, waiting for the
nightmares to end.

That day, still fresh in your
mind after nearly eighty-
thousand showers, three years,
and ten people blaming you in

conversations later.... You are still living in fear even though you are not even in danger.

Why, you ask?

She sleeps a few feet from where every piece of her was left from the first time she was forced to beg for her peace of mind, to be left alone.

No one came then or now.

I spend time thinking about everything and nothing, but I still can't figure out how that day went from pretty good to hell on my own bed, and me wanting to say forget everything and everyone and just end it, but I can't.

No matter how much I
want to I can't.

I was raised through
hell and back.

I knew what physical, sexual,
verbal, spiritual, and emotional
abuse was before the age of seven.

I learned that the words stop and
no are just words that don't mean
anything, that nobody really cares
about what happens to people,
and that some people don't care
about age, consciousness,
or consent.

So, with that being said, she is
human, right? she is alive, right?
she is breathing, right? Her mind
asks her everyday these
same questions.

Results pending.... :
yes, no, maybe, I don't know.

You made this darkness so much
darker and the pain so much
more painful.

I want to breathe,
but I am too scared to.

I see you, everywhere!

Breathe, woman!

It happened. I said stop. It's over.
You are safe, so it's alright
to let sleep claim you.

Seriously

Please tell me: when did
stop ever mean go?

Didn't you ever play the traffic
game? Or were they just
commands that you would not let
form in your mind? For I know
life has a tendency to have those
dark, empty corners, filled with
shadows and body parts crawling
on someone who didn't want
them, who could not ignore the
various mind-erasing screams,

saying stop or no coming from their own vocals.

While the shadows close in and darkness turns to light, we hear the voices of the friends we once thought we knew telling us, "What did you expect?" "You wanted it. " they call us "used mattresses" "Slut" "whore" "bitch", joking with us: "no totally means yes in every way" (wink-wink). "

We are too serious, but please restate, reclaim, and reevaluate the definition of the words rape, sexual assault, sexual harassment, and sexual abuse, for my definition has always been and always will be serious, even when people try to play it down. It still

comes up as if it were
a gravitational pull.

Even if you didn't play the traffic
game, you must have learned that
right from wrong is never a game,
un-less you planned on being the
reason for the pain hidden behind
some one's eyes. If that's the case,
then remember these words:
anybody who lives through the
attacks and pains during, before,
and after is a survivor, and for the
ones who didn't rest in peace and
note you survived too, and I can
only hope to promise that soon it
will be taken seriously.

Women and/or men, men and/
or women, boys and/or girls, girls
and/or boys are forced to wear a

victim name tag everyday whether it be from physical, sexual, or emotional victimization.

And so, as the old saying goes: "does someone have to die to be taken seriously?" If that is the case, can we take the tagline for humanity off now?

SERIOUSLY.

Pain

Pain is not a game.

It is who I am whether I am in it
or just getting through it and/or
the day/days. It is all a past tense
of something or someone, but that
doesn't mean a definition.

The definition or to define....
I am not an experiment or word
to be analyzed and defined.

I am human. No more, no less
So no need to breathe deeper than
necessary as we are all panicked,

trying to rush, never stopping.

Panicked in pain is a tragedy. None the-less, pain is pain whether we feel it, hear it, and/or see it.

It's there silently waiting to strike, so we hide while we can, but it's so hard to hide, especially when we have to explain or try to explain and all that we can hear is the sound of our own voice wanting to ask, "Why are you apologizing? We've gone through more and worse than this. Besides, you don't even really mean it, so do not pretend like you care. "

Until we hear a faint voice that reminds us of who we really are: that we are safe and it's okay to be afraid. And another voice says, you got this. And more vocals chime in and say, there is not anything you could say that I haven't already heard, so please let me help you because there is so much more to you than just pain.

Smile

Smile because things can't
possibly be that bad.

Smile because things do get better.

Smile because you don't have
anything to frown about.

Smile because you're alive.

Smile because someone
told you to.

Smile so you don't cry.

What about smiling just because
you feel like smiling?

Depression

Is an empty, gnarled pit of
numbness and emotions that taunt
you saying such awful things that
you can't even bring yourself
to get out of bed anymore.

It's like you can't do anything right.

You second guess your-self-more
times than a basketball player
makes it to the net, and you just
want to scream, Enough! I want
to be normal again. Until you
remember: -this is your normal.

When there is finally light at the end of the tunnel, for a while you get excited. Maybe now it's over. Then you hear those words saying you are mentally ill, you need to take these medications, and that light at the end of the tunnel turns back into the shadows you are plagued with, and you either take the medication and hope it helps or try to cope without it.

"'Hear me!'" you scream inside as you hear another voice saying, don't say anything or end it, but we don't talk about this anyways.

We sometimes just have horrible days with no explanation other than:- depression.

What Does Life Mean

Life is a shallow existence.

Teeter—tottering on a fine line of
desperations, aspirations, and just
time-consuming necessities.

No time for patience.

Worrying day in and day out.

Never once stopping to take a
breather or feel the sun or
just go for a run__.

A moment of peace, not just
pieces of a moment where I have
to wonder where my heart and

soul and passion went.
My mind set out on a journey
to say, "I am crazy. "

To that I must say, where is my life?

My mind is as it is and
as it will always be.

The sound of life's meaningful
or meaningless glory or sorrow.

Either-/or, life is a challenge in
which some of us are not as lucky
as others: we have it taken away
from us before we know
what it, he, she, we are.

So, before you claim to know what
life is and or what it means or
any other variation that you want
to throw in there, take a walk on
the side that has a slow, simple
tolerance for bullshit.

My Hero

She is and will be a mother, a
sister, a daughter, a friend, a
girlfriend, and a wife.

A woman of many talents:
brains, courage, and beauty.

The woman who cares with
no ulterior motive.

A warrior who has been to and
through battles and came out a
queen with scars that only
make her stronger.

Loving, sweet, kind, and amazing.

You will want to stay on the side
of her that will hold you close
with a knowing will of love, trust,
and daggers for those who
cross her loved ones.

A woman who is a hero to all
and inspires others to be.

A hero draped in a secret life of
freedom, strength, pain,
and herself.

She is the woman you want to be,
but will always tell you to forge
your own way.

She is everything to everyone, so
if you love her then love her, but
don't hurt her because those who
love her have warned you.

Word of Focus for Life

WELL-BEING

DEFINITION

The state of being comfortable,
healthy, or happy.

Focus. Word. Needs.

I need to want this for myself.

I need to follow my gut
no matter what.

I need to say no.

I need to say enough.

I need to be myself.

I need to make a decision
(on my own).

I need to learn how to
ask for help.

I need to stop making excuses
for myself and others.

I need to get out of my house.

I need to stick to my plans and try
harder to be on time.

I need to take better care of my
physical, mental, emotional, and
spiritual health.

I need to get rid of anyone or
anything who is not helpful to my
well-being.

I need to take things step by step.

I need to learn to balance
everyday life and more.

I need to trust less and more.

I need to let go more.

I need to love myself and stop
being so hard on myself.

I need to check in with myself and
maybe ask other people to check
in with me and make sure that I
am checking in with myself.

I need to talk more openly about
my personal and non-personal life
even the topics I usually
say are off limits.

I need to love and help more.

I need to learn how to be loved.

I need to be more sociable.

I just need to focus on
my well-being.

Not That Little Girl (Anymore)

Good girl!

Do as you're told!

You have not been through
half of the stuff this person
has been through.

So worth it ha!

Why were you even born?

Oh! Yeah! Now I remember
you were born to only be there
for others and not ever yourself

even as tears, nightmares, and flashbacks cradle your sleepy-sleeplessness every night pretending they are not real.

You were born to be someone's punching bag and footstool, whispers telling you to hide the bruises, welts, and self-inflicted scars—no one will believe you anyways.

You were born to be someone's this and that, bitch, whore, liar, doormat, body to crawl upon even when they hear stop, a thing to stalk and grope and torture.

You were born to be just something with every kind of victim tag you have been forced to wear wrapped around your throat

so tight they have
become birthmarks.

You were born to be whatever
anyone wants you to be, for you
are worthless and will
never be enough.

But that's just it. I was not born to
be any of those things so excuse
me if I seem a little mean, but I
am in my twenties, and I am just
learning. I am still learning that
I am worth it, so at arm's length:
I need time to just be me without
a leash telling me the how? Who?
When? Where? Why? What?

Normality

Normality, bro!
Where did you go?
Did you even really exist?
Or was I just tripping like a
dramatic soccer player?

I know we were never that
close, but did you have to vanish
without even so much
as a goodbye?

Getting along has never been
our strong suit. Yes, I get that,
but dammit I want us to kick it

sometimes like karma and mother
nature at a how to get back at
your cheating ex/what's new with
your body seminar part two.

Growing
(From Girl to Woman)

The girl who at one point in time cut herself, drank like a fish, smoked 420 style like second nature, and even smoked a few cigarettes just to feel something other than the horrifying pain she was already feeling.

The girl who would eat anything in sight just to feel full of something other than empty, shattered, emotional, and numb.

The girl who would not eat anything just to see if she would fade away or because her stomach wouldn't let her or she would get so depressed she just couldn't bring herself back to reality to be able to eat something.

The girl who would sit quietly staring at people just to see if anyone would notice if she stopped talking, stopped breathing, or more specifically just wasn't there anymore.

The girl who would lie in her bed until she got so cold she could almost pretend she was dead so she wouldn't have to be in pain anymore, but then she would remember to breathe which would remind her that while she is cold, she is still alive.

The girl who would lie on her back or, stomach, or knelt down for people she thought cared about her because she wanted someone to and to be able to feel like someone did and because she was tired of fighting.

The girl who gets crushes on people she knows she shouldn't, so it takes some of the pain and worry away from when it starts to when it is over even while she is in the relationship or whatever it is.

The girl who learned to expect the bad stuff so much that she can see it coming and tries to run but doesn't get far before it grabs her by the throat and soul until she is an empty shell, a husk of a person, and/or a breathless corpse.

The girl who keeps letting people hit her, put her down, hurt her, and make her feel so used, unsafe, and worthless that the only time she can fully open up is through writing and dancing, but even then it doesn't feel like she has truly opened up because she doesn't talk about what happened or she just tries to pretend like nothing has happened or just blocks it out of her memory unconsciously because no matter how many times she tried to say she is actually ready to talk about what has happened, what is going on, and what she is feeling people will nod their heads and say they are listening, but they are not hearing her and every piece of emotion that has been locked away, every tear not cried every dream turned nightmare, every daydream turned scary monstrous flashback, every thought turned into anxious panicked worry. One would think you would finally hear me instead of leaving me to find the leftover pieces of my shattered corpse all over the universe while you sit nodding saying you are listening.

I call bullshit.

The girl who grew up into the woman who is just a different

age than that girl who would try to crumble into herself, but even now that's still not a safe place to be because it's constantly saying she isn't worth anything, she can't do anything right, she is this and that, or because her mind wants her to go back to cutting, drinking, smoking, and having sex with people she did and didn't know or thought she knew and thought cared about her just to feel something even if it's just more pain. It will just be added to the rest later. For now in these moments she is emotional and numb and whatever anyone wants her to be, for she is not really there. It is all just another layer even when she tries to cope by drinking, cutting, smoking and more. There is a way to cope with the coping styles because whether it is someone else hurting her or her hurting herself it still adds to the pain even though she is trying to take one away with the other.

The woman who grew from the girl is a numb, empty, emotional waste of life who everyone thinks will off herself first chance she gets, not knowing that she has thought about it, she does think about it, and she has tried it, but she is not as suicidal at this point in time. In the future, she doesn't know. She knows what it is like to almost die and want to die

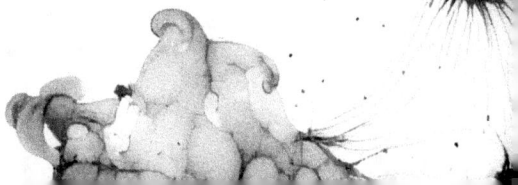

sometimes, but she can say right
now as much as she wants her
pain to end, she doesn't want it to
end like that. She is gasping for
breath as if she was buried alive
other times. She is trying to reach
out to someone or something as
she is falling into a grave
that everyone including
herself helps to dig.

To Little Me

To the little me who didn't know
new days is not just another set
of words thrown together like a
mismatched pair of socks that
people find amusing to
just toss around.

It means something.

To you I don't know I am not you,
nor do I recall asking, but even if I
did would you be honest, or would
it be another anxiety—
filled lie of wonders?

Is that judgment on your face?
It can't be, no, it must not be.
For if it was, I would have to
speak up and say you were just
a portion of my new day.

Hold on I am getting something.
Brain waves shoot to my mouth
as the words flow out. Realization
kicks in: it is the definition of a
new day, stating it is yours, make
it how you want, and if you don't
like it change it because life goes
on without you, and when you
forget how you want it, how to
change it, and that it is yours I
want you to open your brain, eyes,
body, heart, and soul, take a deep
breath, and say with or without.
To the little me: the days when

you wake up just remember that the past helps make your story, but you make you.

When that is safe in your mind, say, speak, scream, however you want to phrase these words spoken loud enough for the masked walls to fall:

"BE YOU & THANK YOU FOR ANOTHER NEW DAY."

I Am Me & I Can Breathe

Every day I wake up hoping and
praying I can say I am me and
I will not be sorry for that
anymore, so do not expect
me to act like I am.

I am done running, screaming
into pillows, and holding in every
part of me. That scared, scarred
little girl grew up.

Reality set in: starting over is
easier than letting go, yet either
way it's hard to do. So that being

Sharliene Phillips

said, I must now say with every
last breath that I am me
and I can breathe.

Making Love

Gently start with foreplay, placing kisses upon the neck of your lover. Then whisper into their ear, I want you to let go with me, no barriers, no holding back, no telling me you reached your peak and you didn't even orgasm, yet.

Trust, patience, timing, and desire are the key words for each and every single time we make love.

The topic and types of love-making styles we have will make

the Kama Sutra blush
and ask us for notes.

Our love-making will be so
powerful that they will have to
create a new type of
gravity around us.

As every part of us rises up to
match each new rhythm set by
the other, we won't even have to
ask for the screaming of names
as other people do. We will just
make love so raw, untamed,
uninhibited, gently, and gracefully
that each of our names will be
pulled out of us like a warrior's
battle cry, so the past, present,
and future will know each time
we make love.

This may seem like a bunch of pick-up lines you hear in a bar, but I can promise you that every single word is the truth of how we will act and what we will do.

So stop holding in that fiery passion as the kisses are being placed upon your neck and those sweet tender words whispered in your ear as you finally let go and know your lover will be there to catch you and hold you even after you recover and are starting the hours over because you both have waited long enough, and it is your turn to be on top and hold your lover and be there even after they recover, for our love-making is a test of boundaries, of trust, of flexibility, and of motion.

It is a dance of unimaginable love, but this is just one case because as they say, I can show you better than I can tell you.

Screaming Pleasure

Screaming, dragging,
bumping, moaning.

All words, all part of life,
but which life?

Let go, be free, scream at the top
of busted windows, letting scents
of sense release from the air as
aromas tingle every inch of every
part screaming out dreams, hopes,
desires while in that moment
of sheer, untamed, insatiable,
heart-racing bliss, every ounce

dissected, every moment
breathtakingly questionable.

Names from corners echo through
halls, screaming, dragging
noises—what is that?
Everything and nothing.

Moaning sighs of sweet low
growls, of desperation, of
orgasms, and angry passion
cornered with ear bludgeoning,
maddening shouts that bust vocal
cords and walls saying "more,
more, more!" Deeper and deeper,
the feelings of excitement form
even closer, and there is nothing
and I mean nothing that can stop
that first screaming, dragging,
bumping, moaning sound of
sweet, sweet desire, but those

final words, until pleasure and passion are no longer just words, and there is nothing more to say. But in five minutes, we will go again. After all, it is nothing more than just screaming pleasure.

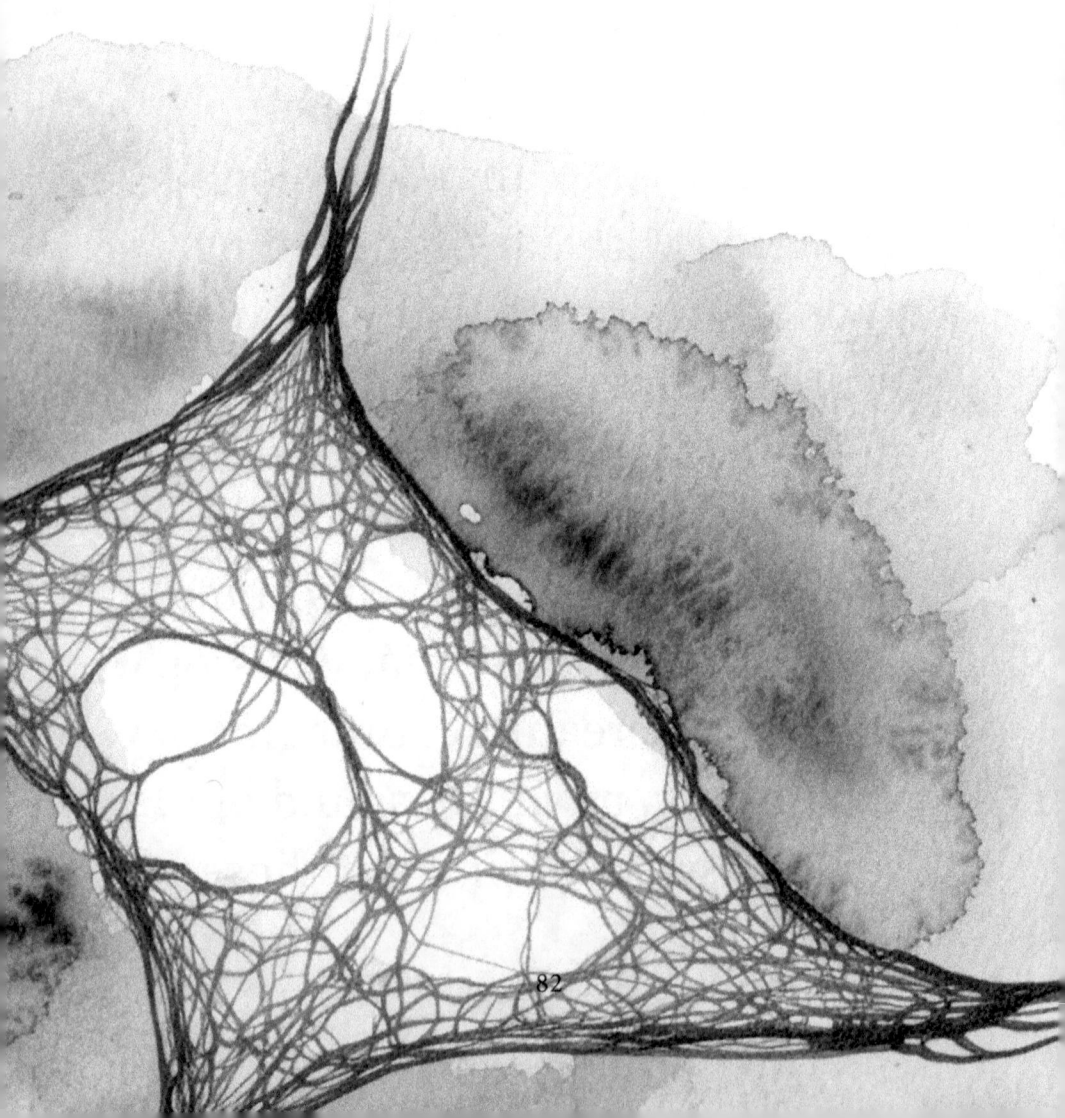

Love for Your Future Significant Other

You know the good, the bad, and the ugly, yet you're still there.

Every time my eyes leave yours it's because it's still uncertain if you will give me something to trip over instead of just letting me fall.

I see you not catching the glances my heart throws your way each time we are near and even more when we are not.

I get that we have to wait for marriage, children, and family, but baby please note that with every breath in me and every breath in you screams for that moment when you and I will finally be. And I don't just mean be as in the birds and the bees I mean hands held, walking down the side walk, sitting in a movie theater, snuggled up, eating kettle corn, lounging on the sofa, feet stretched out, massaged and relaxing, watching poetry videos on YouTube, walking down hallways and aisles of malls and grocery stores screaming _(insert name here)_ is the _ (insert gender(s) here)_ I love

Sharliene Phillips

the _(gender(s) here) who holds my heart every day and every night; reminding me for reasons I cannot explain... (name here) loves me too.

Before I Tell You,
I Am In Love with You

I am in love with you.

For some reason showing it is
easier than breathing, but saying
it is like trying to memorize
each word in every language...
dictionary definition and
all in one glance.

There is nothing more I
would love to do than tell you
I am in love with you.

My heart aches, for just the mere

thought of you, a picture,
a slow sweet gentle... hug.

I miss you when you are at your
home and I at mine, wishing that
I was there, or you were here.

Some days I can sit for hours
picturing the rocking chairs
built for two, laughing and
joking about the good old days
as we watch each new and newer
generation play, but then reality
sets in, and I must remember
I haven't even told you:
I'm in love with you.

Nature

It is beautiful.
It is strength.
It is grace.
It is a wonder.
It is fear.
It is changing.
It is nature.
Nature is not an it.
Not something to be torn down.
Not something to carve love into
when it was already there.

Sharliene Phillips

Nature is life from the broken branches to the first and last petal that blooms after a long winter.

Nature is alive and has been for generations, which is how we are all still here. So hug a tree, smell a rose (without picking it),
lay on the beach and watch
the sunset and sunrise.

It's up to you.

Love and celebrate nature before you become one and the
chance is gone.

Fat

Fat... Really?

Is that all you've got? We have all
called ourselves worse than that,
so let me take the time
to educate you.

Fat is a three letter word people
use to describe either themselves
or someone else in the
rudest manner.

So hear these words flow
from my lips as I say.

I am fat; yes, but not
in the way you say.

The way of the bear who attacks
the pot of honey, not caring what
his friends say about the dangers
of how the bees will see
him and treat him.

I am fat; yes, and in love with
every single wide hip, big thigh,
muffin-topped sway of my
motions, laughing in your face
with a sigh saying don't hate me,
for I love me, and I
know about me.

Know and love yourself, and you
will see why I don't make the time
for your hate-filled words.

I am fat; yes, I am big boned;
yes, I am more to cuddle; yes,

I am everything I say I am the understanding I am trying to give you, so next time you feel the need to toss a joke or two maybe even some hate-filled words, watch me keep going with my head held high saying thank you for your opinion, but I love me.

Anxiety Attack

There is nothing wrong or
is everything wrong?
You can't even tell anymore.
You were just sitting there talking,
laughing, joking around.
Good times had by most minus
the random thoughts about every
single thing, day, and so on; in
the presence of a human that
can no longer hear anyone or
anything anymore, for the sound
of fear cloaks their senses like dirt

around that corpse they found last week. It's not like on TV, but that's beside the point of misconceptions.

This person can not even breathe anymore.

They don't hear you.

They don't see you.

They can not even speak to you.

So even as they long to actually hear and acknowledge those sweet savored words flow from someone's tongue; it's going to be okay, you are safe, just breathe as they are slowly turning into that monkey statue and secretly hide from all the evils they have been forced to see and endure day after day, and every single thing going on with every one of them, but as the breath comes back into your body and you reach for your water hoping no one noticed.

Besides, as many stolen times of shaky, what's-going—on breathlessness moments of anxiety that have gone unnoticed or unspoken of, you keep it inside because anxiety just won't be tolerated, or didn't you know society is perfect so there is no need for anxiety, yet starting from or didn't you know to not need, for anxiety was the only part with sarcasm.

Panic Attack

You can't breathe, your insides are shaking, and you feel like you are going to vomit. What is going on?

Only one answer: a panic attack.

You are frozen and everything in you is saying take a deep breath, count to ten, but sometimes you can't even find the breath to take deeply without nausea rolling it's way up your insides, and dizzy, depressed darkness threaten to consume you, so you tell yourself

to close your eyes. Oh no!
Wait why? Your eyes close
and it gets worse.

Try to make it stop,
so you can breathe.

Your caving—in chest feels
like an allergy side effect of an
experiment gone wrong. Wonders
of the biggest earthquake
registered in history right under
every piece of your flesh lacing
your veins, bones, tissue, and
muscle into its core shaking
organs and all.

Ranting and soft, silently numb
shouts shimmy to my ears as the
breath finally releases the shaking
stiff insides it has come to know;
while you see the panic slink

into the shadows waiting for its
chance to attack again as your
horrifyingly-embarrassed mind
wonders, did any one see
the panic attack.

Educate Each Other

Please, I am not mad when for
the hundredth time someone says
they know more about me than I
do. But since you claim to know
me, please spit forth each line of
my story and I will tell you when
you slip up, and when my turn
comes, I can only hope you
will do the same.

So shall we begin?
Please educate me about me.

You are a quiet,

shy know—it— all with a little bitch complex oh, excuse me did I say that? Oh well, I think I have just described you. Any thoughts or would you like to run them by your complex first?

Well, let's start with saying don't judge me until you know me, don't underestimate me until you have challenged me, and don't talk about me until you have talked to me. I digress though because I wondered quite honestly if you would be like me and use your turn to describe us both. On the other hand, we are similar and different, so that was your way and this is mine.

As I have told people time and time again, you know the outside variations of emotional states. At least, in the off occasion I show my emotions just like you I think, but maybe not, for the person you see before you is just that other person that you claim to know.

So no, I am not mad when I hear someone say they know more about me than I do because you can't even imagine the stuff I have been through, but it was an experience from which I am still learning. As for your experiences, I can't even imagine because even if you tell me about them all I can do is say I am sorry for what you have been through as well. I am

here for you because I am not you,
nor will I pretend to be.

So stop assuming you can educate
me about myself because everyone
has at least one thing in common;
however, that does not mean you
know them or that you can tell
them or anyone else their story.

Starting with
This Generation

Our greatest accomplishment?

Love.

Not just for ourselves, but for the generations who have come, gone, will come, and will go.

As a human as to be one.

If we do not learn to change our views on the view of how yes, we have been through and are still going through times that were

and are horrible and times that
were and are excellently amazing,
then we will miss out on so much;
realizing it or not,
we will miss out.

We say we want to leave
something behind for the next
generation, so we put trinkets
and souvenirs in boxes to let the
earth swallow for another time,
yet we have only encapsulated
our memory of what we perceived
that lifetime to be and that
hopefully the next generations
will do better.

But.

Why the hell can we not
just do better now?

So there will be a next generation...

Who can say yes, I am African-American, Latino, Asian, Indian (both kinds), and every other ethnicity mix, or please check other.

Who can say yes, I am a woman with a brain who can speak her mind... what a shock!, but it is okay because I have this gut feeling that soon you will not just tolerate me, but you will respect and understand me.

Who can say yes, I am part of the rainbow community. Want to join me? I promise I am not trying to corrupt you. I just wanted to show the alliance side is just as fun.

For the people who can-not

speak, someone, anyone, everyone
should stand up and say, I will
speak up for you because you
deserve to be heard just like
everyone else.

Who can say yes, I was afraid,
but I took a chance to learn
similarities and differences in
lives that are changing day after
day by love, hate, and just
plain confusion.

Who can say we no
longer separate.

Who can say yes, every_day
we choose love instead of hate
because the generation before us
finally chose to do better
and not to wait.

Queen

More than thighs to
slide between.

More than hips that make
my twist lethal.

More than lips to feel myself
with sustenance or to kiss
or to pour out my soul.

More than breasts that are for
feeding and also play time.

More than vagina that brings
forth life as well as blood
and orgasms.

More than butt that gives
crap and takes a smack.

You are not a thing to be
disrespected, mistreated, used,
degraded, and downright
demeaned.

You are beautiful.

You are unique.

You are strong, smart, sad, angry,
brave, and an emotion rainbow.

You are a woman and
you are a queen.

Hate

Hate.

Such a word invokes an emotional response that can only be matched by its opposite.

Love.

Hate is a word that should only be used when darkness has your heart and soul in a battle to the death. For the darker your emotions get, the -stronger the hate gets until it wins, and you're left empty and hollow.

The Words

The words I want to use.

Motherfucker.

Jackass.

Bitch.

Shit.

Dick.

Fuck you, off, this, that and more.

So.

So.

So.

Much more.

Sharliene Phillips

The words I am trying to or actually do say.

I am going to pray for you.

Food

Allergies.

Hair.

Past expiration date.

Sensory issues.

Gross, mutant, kitten—head-
looking thing.

Health conditions.

What in God's name am I
supposed to eat?

Dear Firsts

Thank you!

Fuck you!

More importantly God bless you because I don't know how to deal with you now or then no matter how much I try or cry or scream for understanding to deal with whatever you have in store for me, firsts. For we both know this is a battle of caged bloody bones heaped in a pile of soft whispers. Let me out, let me out until the firsts are last.

The Bitter Sweet Release

Why do you cut?
It feels amazing up until you
realize what you did and the
shame and guilt come rolling over
you like a wave crashing
on the beach.
Why did you stop cutting?
It's an unhealthy coping skill.
If you know it's unhealthy,
why do you go back?
For the release.
I need that release.

The Black and Colorful Aura Pain

It starts and ends differently than just a normal headache. Shit, I wish it was just a headache, but no, it's a migraine. You know what I mean. If not, here goes.

Pain. Like on a scale of one to ten, it would be like going to an MMA match with no protective gear and fighting the biggest person with just your head, then your body after a few rounds until your body finally realizes what's going on.

Then, there is the light show with multiple colors and spots.

Then, there is the light and sound sensitivity so bad everything must be turned off, and you hide under the covers and try to sleep it away.

Then, there is the nausea and possibly vomiting.

Then, there is the dizziness and fatigue like you have the worst cold and flu symptoms.

There is so much more that makes a migraine not just a headache. So please, educate yourself.

Medications

What is this one?

What are the side effects?

What's in it?

When do I take it?

Why is that not helping
and/or is it helping?

How much is it?

Is it supposed to do that?
Why and/or why not?

Can I stop it anytime?
Why and/or why not?

Do you have a list because
you need a list?

Is your list up to date?

How many are you on?

Did you set a reminder?

How much water do you need/do
you need water?

About the Author

Hello, my name is
Sharliene Phillips.

I LOVE to write different types
of poetry. The poetry I write is
to touch and free the soul yours
and mine. I live in the US. I love
to binge watch different shows
and movies like drama, romance,
tear jerkers, comedy, and so much
more. I enjoy spending time
with my loved ones.